D1635963

Manners of Love
Life Lessons in Giving and Receiving

Manners of Love
Life Lessons in Giving and Receiving

Joanne Burgess

WESTBOW
P R E S S®
A DIVISION OF THOMAS NELSON
& ZONDERVAN

WestBow Press books may be ordered through booksellers or by contacting:

WestBow Press
A Division of Thomas Nelson & Zondervan
1663 Liberty Drive
Bloomington, IN 47403
www.westbowpress.com
1 (866) 928-1240

Scripture taken from the King James Version of the Bible.

ISBN: 978-1-5127-4087-5 (sc)
ISBN: 978-1-5127-4086-8 (e)

Library of Congress Control Number: 2016907070

Print information available on the last page.

WestBow Press rev. date: 7/15/2016

Dedication

I dedicate this book to the two people in my life who have most clearly encouraged and supported me throughout many years and many endeavors: my mother and my husband. Gertrude Evans Morton, now deceased, was a single parent and a divorcee in the 1940s and 1950s—a time when divorce was unusual and broadly unacceptable by middle-class standards. Supporting a family of five as a food server, a worker in a paper mill and later as a telephone operator, she was the strongest woman I have ever known. Alan Adams Burgess has created a work ethic second to none and a commitment to continued learning in his distinguished career. He has totally supported the effort to help endow a scholarship through the proceeds of this volume. The love of these two outstanding people has inspired me to complete this work.

"The fruit of the Spirit is love, joy, peace . . .
If we live in the Spirit, let us also walk in the Spirit."
Galatians 5: 22, 25

Acknowledgements

In writing these little stories, I have sought the help and advice of friends who have critical insight. I am grateful for the ideas of Mrs. Teresa Bensch, who is beginning her own graduate studies at Lexington Theological Seminary and who still found the time to read many of these stories. I must also thank Mrs. Kathy Elliott, a former elementary school teacher, for her insightful comments about levels of language, word choice in reading to children and placement of inspirational quotations. In addition, Dr. Sandra Matthews, a professional colleague and writing professor, introduced me to readability studies and their value as she offered other specific advice as well. The help of these competent people supported my creating this project.

Mrs. Faye Shannon, a wizard in art and graphics skills, is responsible for the way this manuscript appears. Without her patient and insightful help, this book would never have been completed. In addition, I thank Mr. John Fayad, a book coach, who read and advised me on some of these stories, and kindly offered the title for this small volume. I am indebted to each of these remarkable people for their time, insight and suggestions. I also thank Jenn Seiler of West-Bow Press for her help and information. And finally, I appreciate the four supporters who have been willing to endorse this work: Dr. Faye Clark, Rev. Danny Gulden, Mrs. Sarah Larson, and Mr. Donald Weber. Any errors, however, in this story collection are my responsibility.

Joanne Burgess

March 2016

Table of Contents

Preface

When I first conceived of this little book, I was writing stories inspired by Scripture for an Advent booklet (non-published) that Sandy Springs Christian Church produced for its members. After my retirement, I helped create a scholarship for graduating seniors at that church (2003-2006). A very supportive congregation has enabled that scholarship to function since its beginning, and now my purpose is to help endow it. Whatever proceeds over and above expenses that are generated by this modest volume will support that effort.

All the stories here are true, and I share them with you in honoring the diversity of my experience and the compassion that my friends and family afforded. The stories will generate most interest when adults read them and discuss them with young people. Each story is followed by questions to encourage discussion and a list of vocabulary words that the readers may not know. In a situation in which a word may have several meanings, the definition of the word is given in a narrow sense in order to clarify the specific use of the word or phrase in that particular story.

Part One stories may be useful, not only for reading and discussion between parent and child, but in a Sunday school setting and within reading groups in elementary schools. The four stories in Part One relate to a child's very young experiences. Although the setting may show poverty, the stories reveal gentle and sensitive situations. Part Two stories may be interesting to teens and/or adults.

The seventeen stories in Part Two reflect a variety of experiences across time. Some further relate to family and friends; six others reveal educational and work experiences. "Louise" and "Mr. Ashburn" deal with mental retardation, danger and the need for protection. "High Risk" and "The Request" sound a cry for help, but also show a commitment to move forward against enormous odds. "Uncle Bill" and "Honey" are glimpses of dysfunction in the 1940s. The pivotal story here is "The Invitation," an initiation of change. Finally, "Practical Necessities" supplies a touch of humor.

All quotations from Scripture are from the *Holy Bible*, *King James Version* (Nashville: Thomas Nelson, 1976).

<u>Chickens</u>

"Come, ye children, harken unto me: I will teach you . . . ."
Psalm 34:11

When I was five years old, I didn't know much, but I liked to talk. I didn't have many playmates, but I did have a fenced back yard, so my grandmother would let me play there alone. The yard was never planted with grass and was mostly rock and dirt. When we had rain, we had mud. Running along one side of the yard was a large garden, belonging to a rich, white-haired man, whose recreation after work and on the weekends was working in that garden three seasons of the year. I dashed out into our yard whenever Mr. Arrington was plowing the ground, weeding, and hoping for peace in the process. I liked to walk along our side of the fence and talk to him.

"Hi, Mr. Arrington! What are you planting?"

"Well, I'm putting in some corn by your fence this year," he would reply. "Will you watch it grow for me and let me know how it is doing?"

"Oh, yes," I agreed. "What are you planting on the other side of your garden, the side I can't see?"

"I've got some potatoes, some cabbages, some tomatoes."

"I sure would like to see them."

"Well, I've got to go over and check on them. See you tomorrow."

"Bye, Mr. Arrington."

I became interested in vegetables and tried to look for pictures of them in an old magazine. I wasn't sure what a "cabbage" was. After a few months I was able to ask him if he planted green peppers, string beans, or watermelon. He told me he did.

But there was one crop that I could not figure out. I was completely out of ideas and magazines. And I decided when he came by the fence that day, I would ask him.

"Mr. Arrington, where do you grow your eggs?" I inquired.

For the first time, he stopped and looked right at me. "What did you say?" he asked.

"Where do you grow your eggs?"

He blinked a few times and stopped planting. "Well, we can't have that," he muttered. "Go ask your grandmother to come outside."

Wondering what I had done or said that was wrong, and whether or not Grandma would let me continue to be in the yard when he came by, I raced into the house. Grandma came out immediately.

"Can you lift your little girl over the fence?" he asked. "I want to show her something." Grandma gladly handed me over, probably hoping for an afternoon off.

For the first time, I walked into that beautiful garden and I saw butter beans, potatoes, green peas, yellow tomatoes, carrots and more corn than I could have imagined was in the world. Mr. Arrington held my hand as we walked through the summer house where his favorite black and white cat was waiting for him. Then through the garden gate and into his large, soft, green grassy yard we strolled. Oh wow! The azaleas and roses that surrounded his big house! Next, we passed through the gazebo on our way up to the chicken coop.

Discussion Questions

- What caused the child to look for pictures of vegetables?
- Aside from liking to talk in general, why did the girl talk to Mr. Arrington?
- This story is entitled "Chickens," but what is this story really about?

Key Vocabulary

- **Chicken coop:** a pen or wired enclosure where small fowls, such as chickens, are kept for fattening and producing eggs.
- **Gazebo:** an open or latticework pavilion built on a site that provides an attractive view, such as that of a garden.
- **Recreation:** a pastime or diversion providing relaxation, or enjoyment.
- **Summer house:** a simple, often rustic structure in a park or garden intended to provide shade.

The Performance

"Honor thy father and thy mother . . . ."
Exodus 20:12

The Saturday morning radio show was the only media option in town that allowed children to perform publicly in 1946. My third grade teacher selected a student to go to the local radio station and audition for a spot on the program. Miss Lacke never could remember my name, so she called me "Little Girl" all year. When she selected me to represent her class, she said, "Little Girl, you certainly can't sing, but you are very loud and maybe they will figure out something to do with you." She sent a note home that said I had to come prepared to try out next Saturday.

I had never sung in front of people, and I did not know how to prepare. The radio show would be presented on the second Saturday morning in May, so I started thinking . . . and humming. Then on Wednesday, I walked to the library after school and asked the librarian for some help. I was lucky she had a book of songs. So, we found a song and she sang the tune with me. Then I checked out the book and took it home to practice.

The next Saturday morning, I took the city bus downtown and climbed the stairs of the radio building to the second floor, since there was no elevator. "Am I in the right building to audition for the Saturday Morning Radio Show?" I asked a man at the top of the stairs.

"Yeah, kid. They're right in there." He pointed to a door.

I opened the door, peered in and saw a large group of children, all older than I was. My self-esteem crumbled, but I found a chair in the back of the room.

A balding man with a smiling voice was instructing the group about how to project their voices when they came to the microphone. (Actually I did not know what a microphone was.) Then he asked if anyone played an instrument. One girl played piano, and a boy played a fiddle.

"Does anyone make speeches?" he inquired. An older boy said that he did an imitation of the President.

"How many of you sing?" Everyone else in the room raised a hand, so I raised my hand, too. "Who brought music with you?" No one had.

"Who knows the words to the song you want to sing?" Most of us did.

Then he explained that this was a try-out for the program that would be next Saturday. If a person was chosen to be on the radio show, he or she must come back next Saturday with the music and be ready to sing. He reminded any of those chosen today that they would need to practice during the week to be ready for next Saturday.

"What in the world am I doing here?" I asked myself. That awful teacher made me do it. But then I remembered the song I had practiced so much at home: every time we ate a meal, when I took my bath at night, quietly on the way to school each day . . . and I knew I had to do it. Someone would be disappointed if I did not. So as my hands sweated, I waited for my turn.

"All right, Little Girl," The man finally said to me. (Miss

Lacke must have told him my name.) My knees were quaking as I walked to the front of the room. He found a box for me to stand on so I could reach the microphone. I showed him the words of the song and the lady playing the piano knew the music. So with an introduction of a few bars of music, we began:

> "M" is for the million things she gave me,
> "O" means only that she's growing old,
> "T" is for the tears she shed to save me,
> "H" is for . . . .

That year my mother was all of twenty-five.

The try-out did, in fact, turn into a performance. We reported early the following Saturday morning to the radio building, and the man with the smiling voice rehearsed us several times. He explained carefully the importance of sitting silently while others performed since we would be "on the air." He hoped for a well-presented program of children in the community.

When my turn came, I ignored the blinking signs throughout the studio that announced "ON AIR." When I reached the microphone in a loud voice I asked, "Are we really on the air now?" An expression of horror engulfed the face of the man with the smiling voice as he pounded his head with his fist. We were saved from any further mistakes by the piano player who went immediately into an introduction to the song I would sing. Then I began in my loud and unmusical voice.

I imagined Miss Lacke listening to the program and saying,

"I was afraid that little girl would ruin the program. Oh dear me, what a mistake I made."

However, Mother told me later it was wonderful, and it was, after all, for her.

Discussion Questions:

- What talent did the girl try to show?
- What were some of the conditions that frightened her?
- Why do you think the girl selected the song she sang at the try out?
- In the 1940s and 1950s, children were allowed to have more independent experiences than children are allowed to have now. Why do you think that is true?

Key Vocabulary

- **Audition:** a trial hearing given to a performer.
- **Librarian:** a person in charge of a library.
- **Media:** a means of public communication, such as Radio in the 1940s.
- **Microphone:** an electronic device (instrument) used in transmitting sound.
- **Option:** a choice.
- **To Project:** to use one's voice forcefully enough to be heard at a distance.
- **Quaking:** shaking and trembling from fear.
- **Rehearsed:** practiced.
- **Self-esteem:** a realistic respect for oneself; self-respect.

The Lesson

"Thy word is a lamp unto my feet and a light unto my path."
Psalm 119:105

My grandmother continually sang nostalgic, sentimental songs, such as "Lamp-lighting Time in the Valley." I would hear her as she sliced potatoes and swept out the kitchen. Maybe she really missed her home in the mountains of Virginia. Living in town had certainly been a comedown for her since my mother's disastrous marriage and divorce. She had become simply a baby sitter for my little brother and me because my mother worked several jobs to support us. A semi-invalid, my grandmother often showed insightful ideas. And her ideas took root in fertile, childish thoughts and values.

"You will be nice to everyone but associate with only a few," she told me.

"But, Grandma," I would protest. "I just wanna' go and play with them." She noticed the morals of the neighbors quickly, and I was not allowed to play with the children of families whose teenaged daughters had out-of-wedlock babies. She began humming a chorus of the "Ballad of the Birmingham Jail," and I knew I had lost that argument.

Grandma was a great storyteller as well. In the summer, we would sit on the front porch since there was no television. When day turned into evening and then into night, she would tell us ghost stories about the mysterious swamp lights that lured unsuspecting, imperceptive children, especially young girls, into sink holes. She was a master of the allegorical unaware. I mentally stumbled along until finally seeing that the hole was not simply an opening in the earth. Grandma ended the evening by singing the "Wreck of the Old '97," a ballad about a train engineer who ran his train so fast it jumped the tracks and self-destructed.

When I asked Grandma questions, she often did not give me instant answers. She would say, "I've got to study that one." A little later I would hear her humming, and I knew she was thinking. That was what she said when I asked what to do about the boy who harassed me after school. When we sat down to eat our supper, she said, "Whatever you do, DON'T run away." Later I heard her whistling "What a Friend We Have in Jesus."

I messed up; I punched him. When the teacher's note came home the next day, I saw her read it, fold it into her pocket and continue her work.

After supper, she lighted the lamp, sat down and insisted that I do the same. "We need to talk about light," she said. "When you have a conflict with someone, you can run away, stand and fight or walk away," she began. "Once upon a time, there were two light beams that did not respect each other. One was a sun beam, and the other was a moon beam. The sun beam paraded across the sky showing everything to those below. In addition, he warmed the creatures that he touched. And they loved him for it. The wind and the rain felt inferior to him because they were not always welcomed by the creatures of the earth as the sun beam was. And the moon beam, well . . . she didn't even count when it came to importance in the world.

"The sun beam mocked her, laughed at her and challenged

her to a contest of brightness. Of course, he won. And she ran away and hid in the dark.

"Then one night when the moon beam was sadly shining her very best, the North Star noticed her. From afar, he called to her, 'Little moon beam, can you help me? Will you come up here with me and join other moon beams in order to help me shine down on the earth? You see, sailors on the great oceans and seas of the earth need a point of light by which to steer their ships at night. You can help me be that light. Will you come?'

"Then the moon beam realized that she could just walk away from the arrogant sun beam, and rise to the North Star, where she could be useful and appreciated. And so she did."

Discussion Questions

- What was the main thing the child learned from her grandmother?
- Did the grandmother think the girl handled the problem well? How do you know?
- How should you handle situations in which you are bullied?
- What allegory, if any, do you find and understand in the story?

Key Vocabulary

- **Allegorical**: a story having at least two different meanings, and it can be understood on at least two levels.
- **Arrogant**: pretending to be superior and important.
- **Comedown**: a drop or a loss from a position of importance to a less important job or position.
- **Disastrous**: terrible, sad.
- **Harassed**: tormented, bullied, bothered many times.
- **Imperceptive**: not understanding.
- **Inferior**: less important, less valuable.
- **Lured**: attracted someone to something, enticed.
- **Mocked**: made fun of.
- **Morals**: concerned with judging the difference in right and wrong (good and bad) actions.
- **Nostalgic**: a wish to return to the happiness of long ago in life.
- **Out-of-wedlock babies**: babies born to girls who are not married to the fathers of the babies.

The Visitor

"In those days came John the Baptist, preaching
in the wilderness of Judaea and saying . . . the
kingdom of heaven is at hand . . . prepare ye the
way . . . make his paths straight."
Matthew 3:1-3

John, the Baptist, was a larger-than-life character—part Paul Bunyan figure and part pioneer in his leather clothing, surviving on honey locusts, a trailblazer felling trees. A larger-than-life figure in my youth was my grandfather, and he was really a BIG man. About six feet, five inches and hefty, he always came in an open-bodied lumber truck to visit us because, you see, he was a logger and a farmer. He came to see us in the city about twice a year, once in the fall and once in the spring. Never called ahead, just appeared. Oh, we were always at home. We didn't have a car or any place to go.

What a treat when Granddaddy came! In the fall, he brought us a load of wood to help warm the tin stoves in the damp house during the winter. And in the spring or early summer, he brought vegetables from his garden that we could eat or mother could "put up." We would always help unload the gifts of fuel or food, and then he would take my brother and me on his knees, regard us with twinkling blue eyes and . . . tease us. We were his only grandchildren. He never brought toys; he gave us what he had. For the winter and for our table he prepared the way so that our lives were a little less needy, a little brighter.

An uneducated man, he was quiet, but his presence was noticed. During one visit, when he was talking to my grandmother and mother in the house, neighborhood boys gathered round his truck because it was rare for us to have visitors who drove up to our house. Joe Akers began to kick the truck, and Sam Bruce swung open a door. Jim Flynt jumped on the back of it. Granddaddy saw them and simply stood up and walked outside. The dusty street became as deserted as a cemetery after dark.

Then there was the time he came to visit when my brother had been relieved of his slingshot, a very important possession in those days, by an older boy in the neighborhood. Frank, five years old, was crying. Granddaddy simply said, "Who took it?" He followed Frank into the street, and my brother pointed out the villain. Granddaddy stepped over to him, put out his hand and said quietly, "I know you don't want trouble, son; let me have the slingshot."

As we grew older, we did not see as much of Granddaddy because he grew older too and did not drive his truck to town anymore. But I will always remember his large hands that held my small ones, his smiling blue eyes, and his gifts that prepared the way for us.

Many years later, after I had become an adult and a mother, I noticed that my youngest son continued to grow . . . and grow . . . and grow. He was still growing at 24 years old. And when he turned around to face me one wonderful day, I saw my grandfather in his physical stature, his smiling eyes and quiet nature. God had prepared the way and Granddaddy had made the path straight . . . for someone else.

Discussion Questions

- Why did the grandfather travel to town to visit his grandchildren?
- What did the grandfather do for his family?
- How does God allow us to continue to prepare the way for our families?

Key Vocabulary

- **Felling:** cutting down.
- **Fuel:** wood used to keep a fire going.
- **Hefty:** big, strong, powerful, muscular.
- **Honey locusts:** a kind of tree or shrub having seed pods that can be eaten.
- **Pioneer:** a person who first enters a region to help open it up for others and then settles there.
- **Possession:** something that is owned by a person.
- **Presence:** the ability to be at ease, self-assured.
- **Put up:** to can fruits and vegetables.
- **Slingshot:** a Y-shaped stick with an elastic strap for shooting stones, a toy.
- **Stature:** the height of a person.
- **Villain:** a person who does a bad thing.`

High Risk

"Behold, God is my salvation;
I will trust and not be afraid . . . ."
Isaiah 12:2

When I was a child, my family was one that sociologists today would call "a high risk family." There were five of us who were financially dependent upon the salary of my mother who was a food server. In addition to mother, there were my invalid grandmother, my Aunt Louise who had Down's Syndrome, my younger brother, Frank, and I. Our security was thin and our material comforts were few. We lived in one-half of a duplex along with hundreds of cockroaches. We had no central heat and no hot water. The landlord charged us $12.00 a month in rent. I never knew what he charged the roaches, but during the nine years we lived there, it is accurate to say that he never made any repairs to the place.

It was about a month and a half before Christmas the year that I was five years old. Mother was leaving for work when we heard a knock on the front door. When I opened the door, we all recognized the tall, thin and dour Mr. Means, the landlord. Without smiling, he said, "Is Miz C. at home?" I looked back at my mother, who had been standing in the back entrance to the hallway.

She stepped to the door and said simply, "How are you, Mr. Means?

"I've come for the rent," he growled.

"No doubt you have," she said. "Mr. Means, let's be sure we understand each other. I don't have your rent. If I did have it, you would have received it on time. When I get my salary, you will be paid. Although I have been late in paying, you have always received your rent since I have been living here. You do not need to come to my front door and demand it."

"I'm get'n' tired ov yo' late payments, Miz C., I want my rent now," he threw back at her.

Looking directly at him, she said "I've just told you that I don't have it. But I do have a lease, Mr. Means, and it says that I occupy this house until the year is up. Right now I'd like you to get off this front porch."

He blinked, then turned abruptly and marched off the porch. I closed the door.

.　　.　　.　　.　　.　　.

When I entered second grade, my left-handedness caused a problem for the teacher who believed that all children should learn penmanship with the right hand. She labored diligently with me every day . . . to no avail. I produced only illegible scrawl and tears. My mother consulted a medical doctor and relayed his advice to the teacher, who scowled and informed her that it was not possible to teach writing with the left hand. The next day Mother appeared in the second grade classroom with a letter from a doctor and the principal to help encourage a teacher to allow a left-handed child to write . . . naturally.

.　　.　　.　　.　　.　　.

I was nine years old when I came home from school one day and Mother said, "Take these bags and pack up your clothes. We're moving."

"Where?" I asked

"Across town," she said.

"Why?"

"So that you and your brother can go to a school that offers music."

"But I like my school just fine without the music."

"We will have a bigger house, actually a rooming house, and it will be near a park where you can play."

"But I don't want to go," I cried.

Setting me down and looking directly at me, she said, "Sometimes in life we must do things we don't want to do. The school is nearby, and you can walk there. The city bus will come by our house, so I can get to work more easily. And that park, ooh! That park has a swimming pool." Her tired face smiled, and I smiled back.

"When do we go?" I questioned.

"Tomorrow," she volunteered.

Discussion Questions

- Should Mr. Means have come to the house?
- How did the mother convince the teacher to let the child write with her left hand?
- What was the main thing that the child learned from her parent in all three instances?
- When were you in a situation that required you to do something that you did not want to do?
- How did you handle that problem?

Key Vocabulary

- **Abruptly:** sudden or unexpected manner.
- **Accurate:** free from error, exact, precise.
- **Consulted:** asked guidance from.
- **Dour:** gloomy, severe, sullen.
- **Down's Syndrome:** mental retardation.
- **Duplex:** a house accommodating two families by the sharing of a common wall between them.
- **Illegible:** impossible to read.
- **Left-handedness:** use of the left hand being more effective than the right one.
- **Material comforts:** physical items in a home that would show wealth.
- **Penmanship:** style of hand writing.
- **Relayed:** passed on information.
- **Scowled:** had an angry, threatening look or expression.
- **Scrawl:** written in an awkward, unreadable manner.
- **Sociologists:** social scientists who study development of human society and social groups.

Uncle Bill

"This is my commandment, that ye love one another . . . ."
John 15:12

I never understood him, but he was very good to me. The first night I spent away from home was at Uncle Bill's house; I was three. After breakfast, he showed me his prize tomato plants, and later he let me take one home. He taught me about the Civil War before I could read, emphasizing how uncivil the North had been. When I married, he walked beside me and answered the question, "Who gives this woman . . . ?"

But when he visited my grandmother, who lived with us, he raised his voice. "Mama, what are you doing that for . . . can't you see that won't work? Oh, you don't know what you are talking about . . . ." He was impatient, but he came to see her regularly . . . and yelled. Uncle Bill learned to be angry before I was born.

He came each Christmas and brought her a gift, usually a house dress or a night gown. She was semi-invalid and did not go out. He always shoved the gift toward her. He never said, "Merry Christmas." She never said, "Thank you." He came at Easter and left a lily on the table. There were no remarks about its beauty.

"Mama, you take too much medicine," he would preach. "You've got to cut back on that stuff."

"It's what Dr. Rosser prescribed for me. You are not a doctor," she reminded him.

"I've got more sense than he has, and you know it," he offered in his own defense.

"No. I don't," she shot back and stood up to leave the room.

"There you go, always leaving," he observed. She had left his father when Uncle Bill was thirteen.

Grandma continued taking the medicine. She was diabetic, and later she developed Leukemia. Family members took turns sitting with my grandmother overnight the week during which she died. Uncle Bill's turn came the night we lost her. He held her hand tenderly. He did not yell when she left.

Discussion Questions
- What did Uncle Bill enjoy doing?
- What made him grow to be so angry?
- Did Uncle Bill love his mother? How do you know?
- In what ways do you show love to your family?

Key Vocabulary
- **Diabetic:** having diabetes, an illness involving a person's insulin and blood glucose levels.
- **Leukemia:** a cancer of the blood.
- **Semi-Invalid:** a person whose health is not very good.
- **Uncivil:** without good manners, rude.

Louise

"Blessed are the merciful . . .
Blessed are the pure in heart . . . ."
Matthew 5:7-8

Her name was Louise, my Aunt Louise. She was about four feet, seven inches tall with dark, straight hair and a crooked smile. She was totally trusting and without guile. A woman with Downs Syndrome, she never expected anything, which was a good thing because the family didn't have much. I never remember that Louise got a new dress, or new shoes, or a new coat. Any spare money my family had was spent for a jacket for my brother or a dress for me because we had good minds, and we went to school.

Louise lived with us because there was no other place for her to live. No family member besides my mother, her half-sister, would support her. She slept on a cot next to my grandmother's bed and helped my grandmother, who was often ill and quite often impatient with her. One of her jobs was to get up early before the family arose and start a fire in the tin stove in the bedroom.

One Christmas Eve, the dreadful cold and the howling wind of central Virginia penetrated the uninsulated house after the fire had died down. Mother was working the graveyard shift at the paper mill, and the rest of the family was asleep. Louise mercifully arose at about 5:00 a.m. to start the fire. Taking the poker, she cleaned out the ashes from last night's banked fire, searching for embers from which to resurrect a blaze. Kneeling, she placed kindling wood in the stove and began to blow on the potential. By that time, my brother and I were awake and despite the cold, we dashed down to our small Christmas tree, hoping Santa had not skipped us. We were followed by Grandma, who made a fire in the kitchen cook stove, and Louise was forgotten.

When Mother rushed into the house from work, we were already into the Christmas stockings, eating the tangerines and cracking the nuts. Presently, my Uncle Bill came pounding on the door. "What is the smoke I smell?" he demanded. We had not noticed. We did not answer.

"Where is Louise?" he followed up. Our eyes directed him to the stairs, and he took them, two at a time.

There she was in that upstairs bedroom, now thick with smoke, covered with soot and with the curtains afire.

"What's going on here?" Uncle Bill yelled. "What do you think you are doing? Get out of here!"

When she heard her brother's voice, Louise's fear and frustration with the fire turned to guilt. She bowed her small head and sobbed. Totally on her own, she had set the house afire, an independent act born out of the practice of years of trying to do her best, even in the least of things that suddenly had become such a major thing.

Uncle Bill battled the flames on the curtains, and we poured water on the tin stove. No one ever apologized to her or comforted her, saying it was not her fault that she had been left alone without help. Later that day we all marveled, as people will, at how lucky we had all been in the fire and how fortunate we were that no one was terribly hurt. And Louise, who loved us and brought us warmth, was forgotten.

Discussion Questions

- What problem did Louise cause?
- What was Louise's gift to her family?
- Was Louise punished for causing the fire?
- What should have been done with Louise after the fire?

Key Vocabulary

- **Apologized:** said you were sorry, offered an excuse or explanation.
- **Downs Syndrome:** mental retardation.
- **Embers:** glowing, hot wood that remains from a dying fire.
- **Graveyard shift:** overnight work, for example,11:00 pm-7:00 am.
- **Guile:** cunning or deception.
- **Lack of guile:** simple, truthful.
- **Marveled:** were amazed or surprised at.
- **Penetrated:** pierced or passed through.
- **Resurrect:** to bring to life again.
- **The potential:** what is possible.
- **Uninsulated:** lacking material in walls that keeps a room or a house warm or cool.

Mr. Ashburn

"Keep thee far from a false matter . . .
for I will not justify the wicked."
Exodus 23:7

Well, the name says it all! How would you like a name that says you are all burned out . . . finished? He was a short, little man with a thin, grizzled face, a penciled mustache and slits for eyes. He just walked up with his cane and sat on the porch with us. I couldn't understand why he came at all because there was no man in our house for him to talk to. When he spoke, he wheezed. But often, he just sat there like a tree that refused to give up its last leaves in November. People did that in those days, just being with others. I guess he didn't have any others, so he sat with us.

"Hair you, Miz Ivens?" he said to my grandmother.

"My arthritis is up today, Mr. Ashburn," she retorted.

"Yep. Damp weather will do it," he smiled, but he looked pained.

Louise, my aunt who had Downs Syndrome, was in the squeaking porch swing and he saw her. "Nice chile," he murmured to Grandma as he moved onto the swing. "How you, Miss Louise?"

No one ever asked her how she was, so sweet and shy Louise smiled purely. He moved closer and pulled a peppermint from his pocket. "Bet you'd like one o' these, sweetheart," he said to her. And he lightly pinched her cheek as she took the candy.

"Looks like fall is coming on, don't it, Miz Ivens?" he wheezed. Grandma simply rocked in her chair. "When did this girl go to a picture show?" he asked as he looked at Louise again.

"You want to go to th' show?" he questioned.

Louise eyed Grandma. No response.

"Where you get that pretty dress?" He asked Louise about the faded but clean apron she wore as he touched it. Getting uneasy about the attention she was receiving, Louise began to chew her finger nails.

"I believe the rain is coming, and you best be gettin' long home, Mr.Ashburn" Grandma announced as she pulled herself up.

The small man with slit eyes slowly stood and said, "Well, mebbe 'nother time, Miss Louise. Good Day, Miz Ivens." Then he snaked off with his cane.

Mr. Ashburn came again the next week on another fall afternoon. We were on the porch and Grandma saw him moving slow up the street. "Come on," she said to Louise and me. "We got work to do." We left the porch. As he passed, the wind picked up and scattered the last of the leaves.

Discussion Questions

- Why did Mr. Ashburn come by to sit on the porch?
- How did grandmother protect Louise and the child?
- Would you trust Mr. Ashburn? Why or why not?
- What should you do when someone tries to influence you with candy or promises?

Key Vocabulary

- **Arthritis**: pain in a joint, often in older people.
- **Downs Syndrome**: mental retardation.
- **Mustache**: hair growing above the upper lip of a man.
- **Penciled**: thin-lined.
- **Wheezed**: breathed with difficulty, making a whistling sound.

My Friend

"Judge not, that ye be not judged."
Matthew 7:1

When I was seven, I had only one playmate. Because mother would not allow me to play with neighborhood kids, my only friend was Bennie. Occasionally his mother would drop him off to play for the day while she worked because his father was often frustrated with him. Two years older than I was, he always had the best ideas about what we should play.

We would color with water colors and crayons, and his creations were always better than mine. I didn't care because he was such fun. Sometimes we pretended that we were secret agents, searching for "bad guys." We would run through the house and out into the back yard. We never disturbed my grandmother because she received some extra time for herself while we played well together. The very best thing we liked to do was to dress up in old clothes (usually rags) and pretend that we were the Dolly Sisters, singing and dancing onstage in New York. Bennie would always get my Aunt Louise, who had Downs Syndrome, involved in our game, and it was only at those times that I remember her laughing. Bennie was fun!

Then we moved, and I did not see Bennie for many years.

One day, I accidentally met him on a college campus. What a great reunion! We hugged each other and sat down to talk. He told me what he wanted to major in, if he could just pass the courses . . . and where he was living and working.

"I want you to go with me to see Mom and Dad," he said.

I remembered his parents very well. They lived about four hours outside of town.

So, on a Saturday morning, he borrowed a car from Larry, the man with whom he lived, and we set out. The car had continual problems, his father was not glad to see him, and it was clear that his mother was obsessively worried about him.

Bennie did not laugh as he had when we were children. He made bright, colored pictures then; now he no longer drew or painted. He had ideas about secret agents catching criminals when we were children; now Bennie seemed caught by life. We had pretended that we were successful dancers; now he was neither a dancer nor a successful student.

Life had become more complex and challenging as it always is for young adults. Living arrangements, choice of companions and pursuing an education can present difficult issues. It was good that we could remember a time when the term "gay" had not been coined, but the noun "friend" had been.

Discussion Questions:

- Why did the seven-year-old girl like to play with Bennie when they were children?

- Why was it a great reunion when they met again after so many years?

- Why didn't Bennie laugh as he used to when he and his playmate were children?

- Do you know anyone who seems to have changed a great deal from the time he was a child until he became a young adult? How do you think it best to react to him if he is not hurting others?

Key Vocabulary

- **"Gay":** a common term for an individual who, as an adult, has an interest in same-sex relationships.

- **Obsessively:** thinking about something persistently and unceasingly.

Honey

"And this I pray, that your love may abound yet
more and more in knowledge and in all judgment;
That ye may approve things that are excellent;
that ye may be sincere and without offence . . . ."
Philippians 1: 9-10

It was 5:00 p.m., time for Linda's cocktail, and soon she would start to sing. One could set a watch by it. Linda, a divorcee, and her young daughter, Veronica, were tenants who lived in the rooming house that my mother sublet in 1947. They rented one large rectangular room, which Linda curtained into two triangles: one area for sleeping and one for entertaining. Also included in her monthly rental were kitchen privileges and sharing a community bathroom. Her choice of song at five o'clock, however, depended upon whether or not her "Honey" would come over tonight: a happy Eddie Arnold song for anticipating his visit or a sad Ernie Tubbs song for a lonely evening. He was a large, but quiet officer, who usually slipped in around 8:00 p.m. and out again about 11:00 p.m. The problem was that Honey had a family across town.

Linda was a secretary who worked 7:00 a.m. to 4:00 p.m. each day, adored Veronica and was a little confused about life. She fit right in with the other tenants, some of whom were restaurant servers, beer truck drivers and a newly married couple. The restaurant employees worked late and irregular hours. (It was good luck that they didn't sing.) The truck drivers were often gone for

32

days at a time. The married couple, well, we never saw them. So, the house was a microcosm of ordinary people with limited means.

One evening in September, the tenants gathered on the porch. It was a time when "depression" referred only to the financial ruin of the 1930s. Linda, however, and her neighbors complained together and showed depression of spirit. Allowing envy and frustration into her life, linda said: "Honey's wife, Alma, does not pay attention to her husband . . . she never looks after him. The poor man leaves the house without breakfast every day." Then the waiter shared that he was tired of the long hours working for a slouch of a manager, and the beer truck driver offered everyone a brew that he just happened to have left over from last week's trip.

After Honey's visit the next night, Linda walked with him to the porch. There in the darkness sat a woman. "Hello," the woman said. "You must be Linda. I'm Alma and I have come for my husband."

"Why . . . what . . .?" stammered Linda.

"Good questions," continued Alma. Sincere and without offence, she said: "I have four children, and three have special needs. Tom is ten and was born with a club foot. Doris, a sweet child who misses her father, is eight and has a heart valve condition, and Phyllis, who has impaired vision, is five. These are my reasons for searching for my husband."

"Oh no," rejoined Linda.

"Oh yes," clarified Alma.

So, information from Alma became knowledge for Linda, which affected her judgment and reduced her confusion about life. So Honey never came back, and Linda stopped singing at 5:00, which was good for all of us.

Discussion Questions

- Why did Linda sing at 5:00 p.m.?
- How did Alma, in confronting Linda, help Linda to reduce her confusion about life?
- Why did the tenants gather to complain about their lives? Is that a good thing?

Key Vocabulary

- **Anticipating**: expecting.
- **Brew**: beer.
- **Club foot**: the condition of being born with a deformed foot.
- **Depression**: sadness, gloom,
- **The Great Depression**: the period of low business activity, beginning in 1929 and continuing through the 1930s.
- **Heart valve impairment**: a part of the heart muscle that controls the flow of blood that does not work properly.
- **Impaired**: weakened or damaged.
- **Microcosm**: any group that is seen as a small version of larger and similar groups in the world.
- **Kitchen privilege**: rights or benefits to cook and eat in the kitchen.
- **Slouch**: to sit or stand in an awkward, drooping posture.
- **Sublet**: to rent out.

Jack and Irene

"... Simon Peter having a sword drew it,
and smote the high priest's servant,
and cut off his right ear. Then said Jesus
"... 'Put up thy sword ....'"
John 18: 10-11

In the rooming house that mother sublet in the 1940s, she allowed no weapons. We lived in a transitional neighborhood, but not a dangerous one. Mother assured renters that our house would be quiet and safe, and the rooms were never vacant for very long. One of the most interesting tenants was a couple who were recently married.

Jack and Irene Beard had been tenants for three months. They were very active, coming and going much of the time. Renting one of the rooms that had kitchen privileges, they sometimes cooked ... in the middle of the night. When we saw them, they were often drinking. And Jack had a friend who sometimes slept over.

"Can I help you with those groceries?" Jack asked mother when he saw her carrying large bags into the house.

"Thanks, Jack. That's a big help," mother said.

"You cook for your family. I wish Irene would cook for me."

"Maybe she will when you have your own kitchen," mother reasoned.

"Well, we'll see," he mused.

Jack liked kids. "Be careful going to the park," he cautioned my brother and me when he saw us rush off. He knew we had to cross a busy street to reach the park.

"Yeah, sure," we yelled back as we ran on.

Jack also liked popular music. His favorite song, *"Good Night, Irene,"* often played on the radio in his room. Jack would sing along with the music. He wasn't shy about bellowing it out:

> *"Last Saturday night I got married,*
> *Me and my wife settled down.*
> *Now me and my wife are parted,*
> *Gonna' take another stroll downtown."*

I did not know much about Irene, except that she was pretty and she was always looking for work. When I saw Jack and Irene together, Jack always had his arm around Irene. I thought that was love.

Grandma worried about Jack and Irene. She worried because they lived in the house with us. Most of the afternoons when I returned home from school, mother was working. That was true the day I returned home, and Grandma told me that Jack and Irene had a loud argument earlier. Then, Frank, my brother, and I walked slowly and quietly past their door, but we could not hear any voices. (Having tenants in the house was always interesting to us, especially when a thunder storm made it impossible for us to play in the nearby park, which happened that day.) Later in the afternoon, I noticed that Jack's friend stopped by to see them.

By suppertime that evening, a cold, steady rain accompanied the thunder and lightning. Frank and I ate our supper with

Grandma and were clearing the kitchen when we heard voices screaming, dishes breaking, and someone racing from the house.

Frank and I dashed into the hallway, but Grandma followed us closely and called us back. Then she went to the door of Jack's room. It was open. Irene was gone, and Jack and his visitor were standing in the room. Jack, who was unsteady and wavering, had a handgun that he was trying to focus on the man.

"No, No, Jack," Grandma called to him. "We are a family of peace and we have children here. Guns are not allowed." She spoke determinedly. The intended victim chose this moment to slip away quickly as Jack turned to face Grandma. She stood firm and put out her hand. "Give me the gun, Jack," she said slowly and kindly.

"I'll kill him, I will!" Jack cried.

Grandma continued standing there with her hand extended.

"Irene's left me; she's gone," he wailed bitterly as he handed Grandma the gun.

"Calm down, Jack," Grandma said. "We will work on this problem tomorrow."

Jack sat down on the bed, placed his face in his hands and mourned sadly.

Grandma closed the door, and Frank and I followed her into the kitchen. Grandma telephoned mother, and they agreed that the police should be called. When the officers arrived, we could hear Jack intoning.

Good night, Irene, Good night, Irene,
I'll see you in my dreams.

He went quietly.

Discussion Questions

- Did Jack and Irene love each other? How do you know?
- What problems can you see that Jack and Irene have?
- How did Grandma handle the crisis?
- What is the most important action to take in facing a crisis?

Key Vocabulary

- **Transitional:** changing
- **Mused:** answered with hesitation
- **Wavering:** swaying from side to side

The Request

"Out of much affliction and anguish of heart I
wrote unto you . . . So that . . .ye ought rather
to forgive him and comfort him . . . ."
11 Corinthians 2: 4,7

My father was born with a personality disorder. Consequently, he was often irresponsible and unable to empathize with others. My brother was eleven years old and in middle school when he first approached our father for help. For three years, Frank had a paper route from which he had earned money. However, his route, which was large, was combined with another route; those total subscribers became the customers of an adult route manager. So, Frank was out of a job.

Since we did not live with our father, we seldom saw him. At that time, he worked with our Uncle Dan, who owned a television repair shop. We knew where the business was.

"I don't want to ask him," Frank said.

"You have never asked him before," I reasoned. "It's not as if you are after him every day for money. You need only five dollars."

Encouraged by our conversation and his need, Frank went to the repair shop on a cold, raw November afternoon. Hesitantly, he opened the door and stepped inside. He saw our father in the back of the shop among many table-sized television sets. When he finally looked up, he noticed Frank and frowned.

"Hi," Frank said, sure he'd been seen.

"What do you want?" our father questioned immediately.

"Can you help me out? I need five bucks."

"What do you need that kind of money for?"

"I made the basketball team at school, and we have to buy our uniforms."

"Did you ask your mother?"

"She doesn't get paid until next week, and the rent is due then. She told me to ask you."

"Oh, she did . . . did she?" He had stopped his work and was coming to the door where Frank was standing. "Well, you go up to the corner there and wait until I can come. Don't you come in here again." He pointed in the direction of the corner. Frank left the shop, walked to the corner and waited there. After a few minutes, snow, wet and cold, began to fall. He wished more than ever that he had not come, that he had not asked. He hated him, he hated the snow and he hated the team that he could not afford to join.

After about thirty minutes, Frank saw someone leave the repair shop and come in his direction. It was Uncle Dan.

"Why ain't you in school, boy?" he asked.

"I'm trying to get some money for my basketball uniform."

"You gonna catch yo' death o'cold standing out in this weather. Take this and go on home now." He placed three dollars in the palm of Frank's hand.

Frank looked at the money and then at Uncle Dan. "But the uniforms cost $5.00 and . . . ."

"You go on home now," Uncle Dan concluded. It was a raw day.

We never understood our father, and he could never

understand our needs. We could not see the shackles of his dysfunction but we felt them clutch and isolate him from us. Slowly, we began to understand that when people have a physical or mental weakness, there are no villains and there must be no victims. Frank earned the rest of the money he needed for the uniform and, therefore, became more independent.

Discussion Questions
- What did Frank want from his father? Why?
- What else do eleven-year-old children need from their fathers?
- In what way did the father's difficulty become a positive experience for the children?

Key Vocabulary
- **Consequently:** so, therefore.
- **Dysfunction:** a personal action or behavior that undermines a person's stability.
- **Empathize:** to feel and to understand another's problems.
- **Hesitantly:** slowly, undecidedly, doubtful.
- **Isolate:** to detach or separate in order to be alone.
- **Personality disorder:** mental illness of negative patterns of thoughts and behavior.
- **Shackles:** an iron ring, for example, around wrists and ankles to prevent freedom.

The Invitation

"'But with everlasting kindness will I have mercy on thee,'
Saith the Lord, thy Redeemer."
Isaiah 54:8

When my brother and I were very young, we did not go to church. My mother worked six days a week and then cleaned house on the seventh day, so we were not able to attend Sunday school or church services. I was in junior high school when my friend, Gayle, invited me to go to Sunday school with her. I was delighted and not only enjoyed the Sunday school class, but went with her to the Youth program at the Disciples of Christ Church. I also began staying for church services. Soon, my brother came with me. Adolescents are ripe for new experiences. Their lives are continually searching outwardly and spinning webs in new directions.

At the church, youth programs were filled with Bible study, choir rehearsals, play productions and especially enjoyable Advent activities. Then the regional youth meets presented even more opportunities in growing spiritually, personally and socially. In summer, I was able to attend a church camp for a week—a brand new experience for a youngster whose family could not take vacations.

The Youth Leader at the church was a very gentle lady who welcomed me, observed me and never asked why my family did not come to church. I lived only two blocks from the church, and one fine afternoon in June when grandmother and I were outside, she walked up and sat with us. I was surprised to see her, but I was glad for her to meet another member of my family. We did not invite her in for coffee or tea because we were not prepared for those niceties. We lacked a room to entertain and drinks to offer.

Nelle Stanger, that gracious, merciful lady, taught me to write prayers and to pray them. She involved me in community service and she encouraged me to consider attending Lynchburg College after I graduated from high school. She and the church provided an extended family for me during my high school years, and she convinced the church to offer me a scholarship for college when I graduated from high school.

I enjoyed my friends at that church, and I adored their parents who made time for me as well as for their own children. Carol Lee's father was a magnet of interest to me. When we went to Youth meets outside of town, he often drove us. A man with contagious laughter, his sense of humor was a warm rain for this parched, young life. I never had known how joyful parents could be until then. And, when I was with the group, those parents never expected me to pay . . . for anything. An invitation from Gayle changed my life in positive ways. Experiences of kindness and mercy overcame the harshness of survival.

Discussion Questions:

- Why did the young girl go to church?
- What skills did she develop through the church's Youth group activities?
- What did she learn about parents that she did not know? Why didn't she know these things?
- How does a sense of humor assist a person?

Key Vocabulary

- **Contagious:** tending to spread from person to person.
- **Continually:** regular, frequent action or happening.
- **Niceties:** delicate or refined manners of living.
- **Parched:** dry or shriveled.

Senior Year

"And the angel of the Lord called unto him . . .
And said 'Lay not thine hand upon the lad,
Neither do thou anything unto him.' "
Genesis 22: 11-12

Sometimes, help can come from unexpected places in unanticipated situations that relate to critical times. The year I was eligible to graduate from high school, my mother, my brother and I lived in a small furnished apartment outside of town. We had moved there during the summer, following my junior year. We had sold our furniture because we knew my mother would be leaving the area after my graduation. The rent for the small apartment was less than it would have been if we had rented an apartment in town.

Two days after school started in my senior year, I was called to the Principal's Office. Mr. Black, the principal, looked at the home address listed for me on school informational cards. He asked if the address was correct and when we had moved there. I assured him that it was correct.

"Well, you must go to the high school in that school district," he said. "You no longer live in this school district."

"But I ride to school every day with the boy next door who is also a senior here," I replied. "We share the cost of gas."

"When you live outside the school district and continue to attend this school, you must pay a special fee," he explained.

When he told me the actual out-of-district fee, I knew that

my family did not have that money and that my mother had not known about the fee. I was a senior class officer. I was an editor of the school newspaper, and I hoped that I would be a contender for Class Valedictorian. My head whirled; I couldn't breathe.

"Please," I begged. "I can work during the summer and repay the money. Hold my diploma until the cost has been met."

"We can't do that," Mr. Black said. We sat there in silence. He stared at me while my teenage life crumbled. Then, without speaking, he stood up and walked into another room. I was misery personified, but I had not been dismissed and could not leave. After about ten minutes, Mr. Black returned.

"Is your father in town now?" he inquired, aware that my father moved frequently.

"Yes," I said, knowing that he would not have paid that fee.

"And where does he live?" Mr. Black inquired.

"On Denton Street," I replied.

"Good. We will use his address," Mr. Black said. I continued to stare at him because I knew that I was legally required to list my mother's address since she was the custodial parent. I did not have the strength to mention this to him. Surely, he would have known. Also, I believe he knew that my mother was aware of all things in my school and personal life, and that I was in no danger of disciplinary action letters being mailed to my father's address.

This was the only time that my father was ever useful or helpful to me, but it was enough. It was as if God (through Mr. Black) had said, "Lay not thine hand upon [her]." He spared me a blow that would have been most destructive to my young life. I breathed a prayer of thanksgiving and thanked Mr. Black.

Discussion Questions

- Why can't the student continue to go to the school?
- The student must do one of two possible things to graduate from the present high school. What are they?
- What did Mr. Black do for the student?
- Did he do the right thing?
- Have you ever had to search for an unusual way to solve a difficult problem? If so, what did you do?

Key Vocabulary

- **Custodial parent:** parent with legal responsibility for rearing a child.
- **Destructive:** tending to cause damage.
- **Disciplinary:** requiring discipline or punishment.
- **Eligible:** meeting requirements to participate or take part in.
- **Misery:** distress or suffering.
- **Personified:** represented a condition in the form of a person to show the intensity of meaning.
- **Unanticipated:** not expected.

Undergraduate Work

"Therefore with joy shall ye draw
water out of the wells of salvation."
Isaiah 12:3

It was clear to me years before I went to college that I would be paying my own way. I considered taking two years after high school to work and save money to attend college, but I decided that I would rather begin college right after high school graduation. I was fortunate to receive skills training as a telephone operator during the summer following high school. I would be able to take classes in the morning and work afternoons and evenings at a telephone company, if the college permitted. It seemed to be a good plan, if I could manage it.

I spoke to the Dean of Students, the Bursar and the Housemother of the women's dormitory.

"How will you travel to work and back?" inquired the Dean.

"By city bus," I answered. "The last bus leaves downtown at 11:15 p.m. If I leave work at 11:00, then I can catch that bus."

"When will you study?" she questioned further.

"I will be working four nights each week, so I will have three days each week to study." She was not convinced but agreed to let me try it.

To the Bursar, I explained that I would receive salary every two weeks and would make a payment on my tuition and dorm fees account following every pay period. He reluctantly agreed, saying "I never had a student whose finances were handled in such a manner. The permission to pay in this way for the following year will be based on your payment of the total account, according to plan, by May of the present year."

It was all I could hope for.

The Housemother was a tiny little lady with a birdlike voice. "Oh, my dear child," she trilled with much concern. "How will you ever manage to get enough sleep?"

Or enough money, I thought.

And the race was on. I had given up any thought of extracurricular activities, such as sports and music, but I had aspirations for the Dean's List and I hoped that the winter weather would be mild.

The only person who had not been contacted about the work plan was the night watchman. He locked the gates of the college at ten o'clock in the evening. I returned to the campus at midnight. The first night that I worked, I found the campus gate closed and locked when I arrived. Since there were no cell phones in those days, I climbed the wall.

When I reached the dorm, I had muddy shoes and a torn jacket. The House Mother, who had waited up for me, cried, "Oh, my goodness! What happened to you?"

The next day, she contacted the watchman and they coordinated information about my return on nights that I worked. Both of them worked late to help me.

With support, such as the Dean, the Bursar, the Housemother and the Night Watchman gave me, the personal freedom that the college extended to me, and the work that the telephone company allowed me, I was able to graduate in good health in three and a half years with two summer sessions. With gratitude, I drew waters of support for my education.

Discussion Questions
- Why did the student work?
- Who helped the student attend college?
- Is this plan a good plan for going to college? Why or why not?

Key Vocabulary
- **Aspirations:** strong desire for or ambition for something.
- **Bursar:** the treasurer of a college or university.
- **Coordinated:** arranged actions in a necessary order.
- **Dean's List:** a list of students of high scholastic standing made public each semester.
- **Reluctantly:** not willing to do something with enthusiasm.
- **Trilled:** sang or uttered in a quavering voice like a bird's sound.

College

"And I say unto you 'Ask, and it shall be given
You; seek, and ye shall find; knock, and it
shall be opened unto you.'"
Luke 11:9

I was really excited when I began classes at Lynchburg College. It was what I wanted and had planned for a long time. In high school, I had taken a course in economics, experienced a semester of chemistry, absorbed the equations of algebra, and read Latin for two years. All of this, teachers suggested, would help me with the Scholastic Aptitude Test, by which one might be accepted into college. No one in my family was able to advise me about colleges I should apply to, so I applied to Lynchburg College because of the encouragement of my church's Youth leader, Mrs. Nelle Stanger. I hoped that she would write a recommendation for me, which she agreed to do.

Mrs. Stanger also introduced me to her husband who was Chairman of the Religious Studies Department at Lynchburg College. I was awed by his title and amazed at his sense of humor. With their support, I was accepted. It never occurred to me to apply to any other college. So, a formal rejection would have changed my life because I would not have known what to do next. At that time, the University of Virginia did not accept women into their undergraduate programs.

Lynchburg College was a remarkable and amazing place. The first night that incoming freshmen gathered, we were treated to a comic satire on *Romeo and Juliet*. The character of Romeo was presented by a tall, thin Science professor, Dr. John Mahan. Juliet's character was played by the Professor of Religious Activities, a shorter and heavier man wearing an ordinary head of a floor mop to suggest a pretty woman. Romeo called to his love in a falsetto voice beneath a window while strumming on a ukulele. He was answered with devotion by the actor who wore the mop. How the laughter rang out! The results of this informal introduction to college were a bonding of students with professors as well as a reduction of fear about college among the new students.

There were many memorable classes during the years I was a student at Lynchburg, but two stand out. I registered for a class in European History with Professor Sheldon Van Auken, a Dutchman who was a graduate of Oxford University in Great Britain. He taught by painting a picture for students through his words. Tests in Mr. Van Auken's classes were usually oral and brief. They occurred at mid-semester and end of term, and the material was often taken from footnotes in the text. If students had an interest in pursuing further any topics introduced in class, they were invited to the professor's little home on certain evenings for continued conversation. (This did not affect one's grade.) The process of learning was challenging and invigorating.

I also registered for a World Literature class, taught by Dr. Gertrude Teller, the sister of Dr. Edward Teller who served on the Manhattan Project. She held the Doctor of Philosophy degree from two European universities. Nevertheless, she discouraged large numbers of students from registering for her classes by declaring that students who enrolled must be able to speak either French or German in addition to English. She preferred small classes of committed and hardworking students to whom she would teach great literature. Those students who were risk takers enrolled in her class, despite the fact that they did not speak French or German. In the class, they found that neither French nor German was required. However, a student would discover that Dr. Teller's knowledge was the motivator, hard work was the challenge, and the small class size was beneficial to all.

Because teachers were my role models, I became a careful observer of classroom strategies for teaching and learning. Mr. Van Auken's commitment to motivating and challenging students through the power of his own words and his insistence that students become careful learners were important influencers of my own teaching style in later years. Dr. Teller's reverence for great literature could be seen when she would guide students through the great ideas of literature and then teach them to speak the beauty of the language. Her respect for the written word and appreciation for literature became characteristics of my own philosophy of education. When a young person is motivated to ask, to seek and to continue a search for knowledge, life changes for that person. It did for me.

Discussion Questions

- Is it necessary to prepare for college? Why or why not?
- Why did professors at the college entertain the students?
- How do your teachers actually teach you? What characteristics of effective teaching can you learn from them?
- How is it helpful to have role models?

Key Vocabulary

- **Absorbed**: to take information in and understand it
- **Awed**: filled with an admiring attitude toward someone or something
- **Beneficial**: helpful, bringing personal enjoyment
- **Chairman**: administrative head of a department in a college
- **Comic satire**: making fun of a social practice strictly for amusement
- **Economics**: science that deals with financial matters in producing goods that people need
- **Effective**: adequate in producing a good result
- **Equations**: in math, showing the process of making two groups equal
- **Falsetto**: an unnaturally high-pitched voice
- **Influencers**: actions of a person that have a compelling force on another person
- **Invigorating**: filling a person with energy
- **Motivation**: an incentive or reason for doing something
- **Pursuing**: striving to gain, seeking
- **Risk takers**: people who do something despite the danger involved
- **Strategies**: plans for reaching a specific goal
- **Ukulele**: a small, guitar-like musical instrument

Lessons For The Teacher

"Shew me thy ways, O Lord; teach me Thy paths.
Lead me in Thy truth, and teach me
. . . Therefore will He teach sinners . . .
The meek will He guide in judgment."
Psalms 25:4, 5, 8, 9

I completed my last exam for a BA degree in December, 1960. I started teaching in a public high school in January, 1961. Because I did not major in Education, student teaching was not an option for me. Nevertheless, I was hired to teach history and social studies in a nearby rural county. I would be teaching two sections of eleventh grade United States (U.S.) history, and two sections of ninth grade geography. I monitored one study hall and had a ninth grade home room assigned to me. I shared cafeteria duty and bus duty with the other faculty members. In the first month of my professional teaching experience three unusual situations occurred.

I was excited to be beginning my career, doing the thing I had always wanted to do. But on the first day of classes, I faced two surprises, neither of which I had foreseen. The text book for the U.S. History class had a publication date of 1938. When the students arrived, I told them that we would not be using the present text book. Because there was no text book money to purchase more recently published material, I explained that instead of using the assigned text book, they would be required to take down notes from class discussion, which would serve in place of the text book. When tests occurred, they could study their class notes in preparation.

When the U.S. history students filed in, it was clear that they were sizing me up. I introduced myself, called the roll, talked about the change in the textbook and began asking them about their final classes in December with the former history teacher. I wanted to know what they remembered from their study about the War Between the States. I spoke about the importance of the war and asked if someone would volunteer to review some of the causes of the war.

No one answered the question. However, there was a response. At a silent, given signal, all class members turned their desks 180 degrees around, so that every student faced the back of the classroom. I found myself staring at the back of thirty-five heads. It was indeed unusual but interesting. Never before had I been in a room where I was certain that every person present was challenging me. Fortunately on the back wall there was a chalkboard. So, I walked to the back of the room where I could face them and announced an immediate test on the War Between the States. I wrote three open-ended questions about the subject on the chalkboard and said to the class that the test grades would be recorded and counted in their semester academic average.

The third situation occurred at the first student dance following a varsity basketball game. Faculty members were told that they were required to attend and chaperone. However, a long standing and practical joke at that school was that the existing teachers simply did not attend, purposely leaving the newest faculty member to chaperone the dance alone.

Only students at the school were allowed into the dance, but on that evening, a tall, rugged, chain wearing, bearded young man in motorcycle boots and riding a Harley insisted upon being admitted. I stood as tall as possible and told him he could not enter. No doubt I sounded like "the mouse that roared." After about fifteen minutes of attracting attention he left, only to go outside and climb the building.

The only other adult on the school property that evening was a man from the local Rotary Club who volunteered to walk the grounds during evening activities at the high school. A student told me that he had seen Mr. Kent earlier, and he offered to find Mr. Kent and tell him that we had a problem that the new teacher could not handle. He came immediately and skillfully ushered the outsider down from the building and off the property.

I was a naïve and trusting young teacher with a great deal to learn. I never reported these situations to any of my superiors. As an insecure, new teacher, I handled the text book and classroom situation as well as I could. But I was totally incapable in the socially unstructured teen-age world.

Discussion Questions

- What are the problems in teaching a history class with an outdated text book?
- Why did the students turn their desks away from the teacher?
- How would you have handled that problem?
- How was the fact that the teachers did not come to the dance a danger?

Key Vocabulary

- **Chaperone:** The duty of keeping order at a young people's social gathering
- **Naïve:** Showing a lack of experience or judgment

The Angst of Education

"For mine anger is turned Away from him. I will be as
the dew unto Israel: he shall grow as the lily . . . ."
Hosea 14: 4-5

It was my first year of teaching. I was working with high
school freshmen, juniors and seniors. Lack of discipline in
the old, wooden fire trap of a building was legendary in the
community. The only enforcer of discipline was Mr. Jacks, the
Principal, *if* you could find him.

"You're the worst teacher I evah had!" Bob yelled and threw
his papers on my desk. I was so angry I could have choked him.
I marched him down to the principal's office. I explained the
reason for our visit.

"You swear at your teacher, boy?" asked Mr.Jacks.

"Yes, sir." Immediately, the palm of the man's right hand
plastered itself sharply to the side of the boy's face and head. As
he put his hand up to protect that side, the man's other hand
swung away from his body and slapped the other side of the
boy's face and head, again catching him unaware.

"OH! OH!" the boy cried and tears flowed down his face.
We returned to class. I had won. Bob was chastised.

I had never seen that punishment before. Actually, I wasn't
sure what it was that I had seen. It really hurt because the
seventeen-year-old would never have cried in front of me if
he could have prevented it. I read up on boxing ears, dreamed
about it, thought a long time about it and about Bob. I had been

so angry with him until . . . I saw the punishment. But it wasn't over for Bob, and it wasn't over for me. He continued to resent me and was more convinced than ever that I was not very good at my job.

It was a month later on a spring afternoon that Bob decided to start a fire in the back of the classroom. I waited by the door as my students streamed out of the building, grateful for a break in routine. Bob came by last, grinning.

"Hold up a minute, Bob," I said, blocking his way and looking steadily at him. "I know you started it. Now, I want you to help me put it out."

His face lost the grin. "You saw me?" he asked. "And you want me to help you?"

"Yep," I said. "Let's do it." We hurried to the back of the room and tried to stamp out the flames.

Hallway noise caught our attention. As we looked up, Mr. Jacks was coming through the door with a hose and water. "What happened in here?" he questioned sternly.

"A mistake," I said. "But, fortunately, we have a future fireman right here to help us."

Although I was strong in the subject matter of my profession, years would come and go before I understood the similarity in growing flowers and growing students.

Discussion Questions

- What caused the student trouble?
- What do students who act out in class usually want?
- What did the teacher do that she regretted? Why?
- What did the teacher learn?

Key Vocabulary

- **Angst:** a feeling of anxiety or anguish
- **Chastised:** punished
- **Discipline:** behavior and order maintained by a system of rules
- **Enforcer:** a member of a group who sees that all members of the group follow the rules
- **Routine:** customary or regular procedures or activities

Jesus and Teaching

"And in the day time he was teaching in the temple . . . and all the people came early in the morning to him in the temple . . . to hear him."
Luke 21: 37-38

I can't compare my teaching to that of Jesus, but I did teach *early in the morning* in New Jersey in the 1960s. My classes started at 7:30 a.m., when it was still dark outside. People voluntarily came early to hear Jesus, but the State Legislature mandated my audience, who would have rather slept in. It's hard to wake up to a discussion of adverbs.

What did Jesus offer his audience that I did not offer mine? Well, a great deal . . . especially eternal life, but . . . what did He say to them that I did not? He said that they should free themselves from the cares of this world.

I said, "Do your homework."

He said, "Follow me."

I said, "Stay in school until you graduate."

Jesus admonished his listeners to consider an insignificant mustard seed that can mature into magnificence.

I said, "Think of your future. How can you make a living? How can you make a life? Verbs are important."

It was a different time in history, of course. But riding on the ideas of Jesus Christ was a quality of life that people wanted. He gave his audience a new sensitivity to their lives and how to live those lives. My audience yawned because many came without breakfast and not enough sleep. Writing paragraphs was not exciting to them.

The audience of Jesus was hungry for understanding and starved for hope. They received attention and kindness from him and examples for creating goodness, as well. But didn't my audience need the same things? Yes, many did. But was I prepared to teach those things? My job was to explain complete sentences, verbs and idioms. It was definitely not the important message about how to live that Jesus, the Christ, taught.

Jesus gave lives depth and quality. I offered basic educational skills. Jesus' audience needed to grow; my audience needed to grow up. Now, about that mustard seed . . .

Discussion Questions
- What did Jesus advise those who came to hear him?
- What did the young teacher advise her students?
- Why are both kinds of advice important rules to live by?
- How does the mustard seed relate to what both Jesus and the young teacher talked about?

Key Vocabulary
- **Idiom**: a grammatical expression in one language that does not translate smoothly and clearly into another language
- **Mandated**: an order or law that required students to attend school
- **Sensitivity**: understanding and responsiveness

What Children Want

"When Jesus . . . saw his mother and the disciple
standing by . . . he saith unto his mother
'Woman, behold thy son!' Then saith he
to the disciple, 'Behold thy mother!'"
John 19:26-27

After I retired, I volunteered in the state Juvenile Justice system for five years. As a volunteer, I served on a panel of citizens who assisted the juvenile judge in placing children eighteen years and younger into a stable environment when their parents were unable to create a safe place for them. For a child to stay with the parent, the parent was required to provide a bedroom for the child, adequate food and clothing, and education. When parents were unable to provide these basic necessities, the juvenile judge decided where the child should live and be educated. Some children were placed in foster homes, and some were placed in group homes, often operated by religious organizations. The citizen panel reviewed the written reports on the family, discussed the case and recommended to the judge what it considered the best placement for the child. The child was always interviewed and was always asked what he or she would prefer, if he or she were over five years old.

Betty Jo was twelve. The social worker brought her to the panel interview. A tall, thin girl with eyes too serious for a child her age, she appeared frightened. Seeing and being seen by the panel was another ordeal for an already unhappy youngster.

"How are you today, Betty Jo?"

"Aw right," she answered without looking up.

"Where do you go to school?"

"Dunellen Middle," she offered without smiling.

"And what grade?"

"Six."

"Who do you live with?" the inquiring panel member asked.

"My Gran-maw, an' I got three brothers."

"How old are they?"

"They thirteen, 'levan and five."

"Where do they go to school?"

"Kevin, he thirteen, most time, don't go. Maurice, he eleven, go sometimes. Kenny, he five, stay home with Gran-maw."

"Why do you think you are here, Betty Jo?"

"'Cause Mama left, didn't come back."

"Are you a good girl for your grandmother? Do you help her?"

"Yes 'um."

The interview ended when the panel member asked with whom Betty Jo wanted to live.

"Mama."

"Thank you, Betty Jo. You continue to help your grandmother now."

Another interview followed the one with Betty Jo. Tommy was six. He was dressed in short, faded pants and a tee shirt. He was ushered into the room by the social worker who told him that we were the nice people who wanted to see him and that he should answer our questions. He did not raise his eyes. Instead, he squirmed in the chair, leaving one foot on the floor.

"You are a nice, big boy for six years old," began the inquiring panel member.

No answer.

"What grade are you in, Tommy?"

No answer.

"Can you tell the lady what grade you are in?" asked the social worker.

"First," he whispered.

"Do you like school, Tommy?"

"No," he frowned.

"What do you like to do?"

"Ride on my skate board," he replied.

"Who do you live with, Tommy?"

"Uncle Bob."

"Where do you want to live?"

"With Mama."

"Well, if that does not work out for you, then who do you want to live with?"

"Nobody," he whispered as he squirmed in his seat and bit his finger nails.

"Thank you for coming in to talk to us today, Tommy."

The children left the room … and then the memories flooded back … I was eleven years old the first summer that I worked a five-day week. The day started at 6:30 AM and ended at 4:30 PM. I kept two little girls while their mother worked. The girls, Julie, who was six years old and Shirley, who was three years old, were not happy children. Their parents were divorced, and their mother was not very patient with them.

After Annie, the mother, left for work each morning, I

cleaned and tidied up the tiny house. Then I made breakfast for Julie and Shirley, who awoke about 8:00. On sunny days, the schedule was always the same. Breakfast, getting dressed, walking to the park, playing dodge ball, racing, and playing "Sorry" or checkers at the community house. Then we went home for lunch, which was P.B. and J. sandwiches. Naps followed. Then we played Jack Rocks or took walks. There were no pools to swim in, but we ended the day with baths. When it rained, we lost the trip to the park, but we read stories during the afternoon.

What seemed as if it should have been an easy summer for little girls who had no prospects for vacation but who had an easy caregiver, was an extremely frustrating time for them. When Julie awoke each morning, she came quickly into the kitchen, saw me and began crying. She would not be consoled. She ate sparingly and returned to her room to be alone with her tears. When Julie began crying, Shirley continually asked, "Where's Mommie?" After a few weeks, that question changed to "I want Mommie!"

No offers of a toy, a ride on a see-saw at the playground, a special hop-scotch game or a favorite book satisfied the girls. Ice cream distracted them for just a few minutes. When they took a break from their tears, there still were no smiles or happy childhood songs. They fought with each other. There was a hunger deep within each child that was not satisfied.

What children want are their mothers and the undivided attention of their mothers. Regardless of the mother's condition, the child will want and will choose to be with the mother even if the mother cannot meet the child's needs. Betty Jo, Tommy,

Julie and Shirley hungered for the close personal touch of their mothers that no one else could satisfy. When the juvenile judge decided on a place where Betty Jo and Tommy would be living that would be more stable for each of them, the children would be forced to live there. But they would not be contented and happy, and they probably would not be able to understand their mother's inability to be with them. All would grow up with a gnawing anger inside each in the vessel in which love was meant to grow. Significantly, the last act of Jesus was to recognize the importance of the mother-child relationship.

Discussion Questions

- What is the value of having a juvenile justice system that helps children?
- What kinds of problems can such a system solve?
- Why can't the system solve all the problems the children have?
- What do you think parents who are sick can do to help themselves and their children?

Key Vocabulary

- **Juvenile:** relating to children
- **Justice:** legal process of ensuring fair treatment
- **Frustrating:** upsetting
- **Sparingly:** very little

Practical Necessities

"Let your light so shine before men
That they may . . . glorify your Father . . . ."
Matthew 5:16

A local social service agency has been important to me since I first read about its mission many years ago. The program at the agency has grown over time to better meet the needs of the increasing numbers of people who require financial and social help.

Supporters of this agency are encouraged to contribute food and useful personal items as often as possible. For better or for worse, I have a practical mindset. I try to contribute each Wednesday because that is Senior Citizens' Day at the grocery store which allows an extra discount, and I can convince my husband that I am being frugal.

Over the years, I have insisted on buying necessary and lightweight packages because of the lack of adequate parking at the agency. So, I may be walking a block or two to deliver the contribution. But the interesting part concerns the reaction of the grocery store cashiers when I come through the check-out line with my products. I can hear quiet remarks, such as "Here she comes again . . . wonder what's wrong with that old woman . . . that old babe *needs* a discount . . . some people are full of it . . . ."

Still, I soldier on, seldom making an explanation or an explosion. Once I tried with a smile to murmur, "I buy for a food pantry," and I heard a sniveling check-out clerk mutter, "Yeah . . . right." I guess it sounded like an excuse anyway after all these years. But slings and arrows of indignity will make no impression on this old woman although I do lower my eyes from time to time.

I try to focus upon the broad needs of the increasing numbers of poor people and remember the times as a child when my own family walked up and asked for help. In an era when there were no food stamps, "corn cobs" had a special meaning. Today, I know I have done a good deed when the volunteer in the food pantry smiles and says, "Here comes the toilet paper lady!"

Discussion Questions
- Why did the woman buy toilet paper for the agency?
- What in the woman's background caused her to contribute to the food pantry?
- Why did the grocery store cashiers react as they did to the woman and her purchases?
- Were the remarks funny? How do they compare to the remarks of the volunteer at the agency?
- How difficult or easy is it to be funny and also kind?
- What makes the difference in being funny and kind, and being funny and unkind?

Key Vocabulary
- **Agency:** an organization that provides service; a welfare agency, for example
- **Financial:** relating to money matters
- **Mission:** self-imposed duty, task or plan
- **Slings and arrows of indignity:** insults, unkind remarks
- **Sniveling:** whining or pretend weeping

Printed in the United States
By Bookmasters